Con KV-684-001

Above: Jonathan Swift.
Right: Hoey's Court,
Swift's birthplace.

O'BRIEN JUNIOR BIOGRAPHY LIBRARY No. 5

Jonathan Swift
The Man Who Wrote *Gulliver*

Controversial and colourful, Swift was the most popular man in Ireland in his day. He was a writer, satirist, friend of the poor, founder of St Patrick's Hospital, dean of St Patrick's Cathedral. Nowadays he is best remembered as the author of *Gulliver's Travels*, a world famous classic.

Media Reaction to the Series
'Short, entertaining and full of great pictures'
The Irish Times

'Easily digestible for young impatient readers'
Sunday Tribune

'Lively, informative, easy to read
and fully illustrated'
Young Citizen

THE AUTHORS

MARY MORIARTY
Lives in Dublin with her husband and three children. She took a degree with the Open University in arts and has taught in the Adult Literacy scheme in Dun Laoghaire.

CATHERINE SWEENEY
Took a degree in arts at UCD. Has worked as a teacher at secondary level and as a translator. She lives in Dublin with her husband and children.

Books in this series

No. 1 Wolfe Tone
Tone, the most famous of the United Irishmen,
secured French aid to help bring democracy
and freedom to Ireland.

No. 2 W.B. Yeats
Ireland's best-loved poet, winner of the
Nobel Prize for literature.

No. 3 Granuaile
Chieftain and pirate, the terror of the western
seas during the reign of Elizabeth I.

No. 4 Bob Geldof
Rock musician who united the world for a day in
the cause of famine-starved Ethiopia.

No. 5 Jonathan Swift
Writer, satirist and beloved dean of
St Patrick's Cathedral, Dublin.

Forthcoming:

No. 6 Markievicz
The 'Rebel Countess' who believed in Irish nation-
alism and fought in 1916. Strong supporter of
women's rights, and first woman elected to the
Westminster parliament.

JONATHAN

First published 1990 by The O'Brien Press Ltd.,
20 Victoria Road, Dublin 6, Ireland.

10 9 8 7 6 5 4 3 2 1

British Library Cataloguing in Publication Data
Moriarty, Mary
Jonathan Swift. – (O'Brien junior biography library:
ISSN 0790-9645)
I. Title
823.5
ISBN 0-86278-210-4

The authors and publisher wish to thank the
following for permission to reproduce illustrative
material: The governors of St Patrick's Hospital pages
6 (top), 71 (top & bottom); The British Museum page
25; The Irish Times pages 47 and (Pat Liddy) 69;
The National Gallery of Ireland pages 15 and 27;
The National Library of Ireland pages 6 and 12;

Typeset at The O'Brien Press in Avant Garde
and Bookman
Cover design: The Graphiconies, Dublin
Cover Separations: The City Office, Dublin
Printed by The Guernsey Press Co. Ltd., Guernsey,
Channel Islands

Jonathan Swift was the most famous person in Ireland during his lifetime. He was known for his work in politics, for his writing and for his charity to the poor. Today he is best known as the author of a wonderful book called *Gulliver's Travels*. This book has been read and enjoyed by different generations of adults and children for over two hundred years.

Swift was born in Dublin in the year 1667. He was born in a street beside Dublin Castle called Hoey's Court. The houses and most of the street have long since disappeared but you can still find a street sign indicating what is left of Hoey's Court.

Jonathan Swift's father was an Englishman and a lawyer. He had come over to Ireland with his brothers in 1660. This was a very important year; it was called the year of the Restoration. Oliver Cromwell, the man who had ruled England for nine years was now dead and the English people had asked Charles II, the heir to the English throne, to come back from France to be their ruler. So the monarchy was 'restored'. In Ireland many people who had lost their lands under Cromwell were hoping to get them back, now that a king was again in power in England. So there was plenty of work for people connected with the law. Courts were kept very busy sorting out people's claims to land. Swift's father and his uncles all got jobs in the law courts in Dublin.

In 1664 Swift's father married Abigail Errick. Her parents had come from England to settle in Ireland in the 1630s. In 1665 the Swifts had a daughter called Jane. In the spring of 1667 Swift's father was taken ill and died. This, sadly, was seven months before his son, Jonathan, was born. Swift, therefore, never knew his father. His mother now had to depend on the generosity of her late husband's brothers to look after her and her two children.

A strange thing happened when Jonathan was only a year old. He had a nurse, an English woman, who was devoted to him. One day a message came for the nurse telling her that a close relation of hers was dying in England. She wanted to see this person again but she also did not want to be parted from the small baby she was looking after. After some consideration she wrapped the baby up well, stole away out of the house and took him with her on a ship to England.

Sea travel in those days was very dangerous. Ships were often shipwrecked or forced by storms to stay for weeks in strange ports. When Jonathan's mother discovered that the nurse and her baby were gone she sent a message to the nurse to stay in England and not to risk another sea crossing with the baby until he was bigger and stronger. And so Jonathan spent the next three years in England. His nurse looked after him well and when he returned to Ireland he was able to read.

STUDENT DAYS

At the age of six Swift was sent off to boarding school to Kilkenny College. His mother and sister now went to England and settled there, in a town called Leicester. Jonathan spent eight years at Kilkenny College and entered Trinity College, Dublin, at fourteen years of age. This was the normal age to go to university as the courses there at that time were more at the level of our secondary education than our present day university courses.

Swift was far from a model student at Trinity. He worked at the subjects he was interested in, history and poetry, but did not bother much with the rest. In those days students had to attend religious services every day as well as classes. Swift often skipped both and had to pay fines as punishment.

At that time, Narcissus Marsh was the Provost of Trinity College. He was responsible for building the first public library in Ireland. Marsh's Library is situated beside St Patrick's Cathedral in Dublin and has remained more or less unchanged since Swift's time. It can still be visited by the public today.

Swift did not like Marsh. This is not surprising considering the number of times the young student got into trouble while he was at Trinity. Swift described Marsh in the following way: 'He has the reputation of most profound and universal learning; this is the general opinion, neither can it be easily disproved. An old rusty iron chest in a banker's shop, strongly locked and wonderfully heavy, is full of gold; this is the general opinion, neither can it be disproved, provided the key be lost.'

In spite of everything, Swift managed to get his degree and he decided to stay on for a further course of study. His plans had to be abandoned however because of the political situation in Ireland at the time.

TWO KINGS FIGHT FOR THE THRONE

James II, a Catholic, had become king of England in 1685, after the death of Charles II. Soon after he became king he started to dismiss Protestants from the top positions in the government, the army, the courts and the universities and to replace them with

Catholics. Catholics made up only 1 per cent of the English population, so naturally many people did not like what James was doing. In 1688 some of the leading men in England decided to ask a Protestant prince to come and take over as ruler instead of James. This prince was William of Orange, married to James's daughter Mary.

In Ireland the native Irish population, who were mainly Catholic, wanted James to remain king. The Protestant people in Ireland however were terrified at the idea of Catholics getting into power. Over the previous hundred years, after various rebellions, a lot of land had been taken from the Catholic native Irish and given to Protestant settlers. These Protestants were now afraid that they would lose their lands if Catholics got into power. The population of Dublin at this time was mainly Protestant and they were afraid that they would lose their possessions and positions of power if James remained as king. So the year of 1688 was a very tense time in Dublin and throughout the country. All during the summer rumours were buzzing about the invitation to William of Orange. People did not know whether to believe the rumour or not and whether William would come or not. The speculation ended when the news reached Ireland that William had landed in England on 5 November.

In those days news could only be carried as fast as a person could travel and the pace of travel was very slow. If the winds were right and there were no storms, a person could travel by ship and horseback from Dublin to London in seven days. In bad weather the journey could take much longer. The news of William's landing probably reached Dublin towards the middle or end of November. It might have been the cause of Swift getting into more trouble in Trinity.

Swift, being a Protestant, would have been delighted with the news of William's landing. Perhaps it was the good news together with the fact that his twenty-first birthday occurred in November 1688 that caused him to throw a party. His celebration must have got out of hand however because on 30 November he was accused of creating a 'tumult' in the college and of insulting one of the staff, the junior dean. As a result he had to kneel down in public before the dean and beg his pardon.

Shortly after William's arrival in England, James was deserted by most of his key men. Even his daughter, the Princess Anne, left him to go and join her sister's husband, William of Orange. Deciding that his case was hopeless, James slipped away on a fishing vessel to France in December 1688.

The army in Ireland refused to accept William as king and remained loyal to James. The tension in the country was now very high. It was obvious that William would have to come to Ireland with an army to try to establish his control over the country. In February 1689, frightened for their own and the students' safety, the authorities in Trinity College closed the university to allow anyone with contacts or family in England to travel there 'for better security'. Along with many others Swift left Dublin for England. He went to stay with his mother in Leicester.

In March James arrived in Ireland. He had decided that if he could defeat William in Ireland with the help of the Irish army, he would be able to regain his position as king of England.

By the end of March James's army was in control

King William leading his troops at the
Battle of the Boyne.

of the whole country with the exception of the cities of Derry and Enniskillen. In April James led his army northwards to capture Derry. Derry was completely surrounded by the town walls and the only way to get into the town was either by sea or through the town gates. When the town council under their governor Robert Lundy heard that James's army was approaching, they considered surrendering the city to James. But some young apprentices rushed down to the main gates and slammed them shut in the face of the oncoming army. James and his army then decided to starve the city into submission. By camping outside the city walls they prevented food getting into Derry by land. They cut the city off from the sea by placing across the River Foyle a boom made of beams studded with iron clamps and held together by thick rope. They laid siege to the city for three months. They were unsuccessful, however, because on 30 June 1689 English ships broke through the barriers placed across the river and brought food and ammunition to the starving people. Realising that it was impossible to capture the city, James's army withdrew.

William arrived with his army in June 1690 and a battle – the Battle of the Boyne – was fought between the two armies on 12 July. The battle raged all day but by the afternoon it was obvious that William's army was the stronger. When James saw the way the battle was going he gathered up a few followers and fled from the battlefield. The story goes that when he reached Dublin the wife of the leader of the Irish forces met him and asked how the battle was going. Ashamed of the fact that he had fled, he blamed his army, and told her, 'My Irish troops ran away'. The lady was not deceived and she promptly replied, 'Then it appears, Your Majesty, that you have won the race.' After James's departure the spirit left the Irish army and they were defeated. This battle ended James's hopes of returning to England as king.

MOOR PARK

In the meantime Swift had got himself a job in England. He was working as secretary and personal assistant to Sir William Temple. Temple was a friend of the Swift family. At one stage of his life he had been very active in politics, but he was now retired and was writing his memoirs. He needed someone to help him with his writing and research, and he hired Swift as an assistant. So the young graduate went to live with the Temple family in their beautiful mansion at Moor Park.

At this time Swift wrote his first poems and sent them to John Dryden, one of the most famous poets at the time. Dryden was a distant relative of Swift's and the young man hoped for a favourable opinion of his poems. He was disappointed, however. Dryden sent the poems back with the comment 'Cousin Swift, you will never be a poet!'. Swift was very hurt and never forgave Dryden.

When Swift came to live at Moor Park an eight-year-old girl called Esther Johnson was living there. She was the daughter of the housekeeper and a great favourite in the household. Sir William and Lady Temple were particularly fond of her. None of their own children had survived and most of them had died in infancy. Esther was born two years after their last little daughter had died so, in a way, she probably took the place of their own children. Swift also became very fond of the little girl. He liked

Esther Johnson, or Stella, as Swift called her.

taking part in her education, teaching her and explaining things to her. He called her 'Stella'.

It was while he was at Moor Park that Swift got the illness called Ménière's disease. He would feel ill and giddy and suffer from deafness. For the rest of his life Swift got regular attacks of this disease.

Although Swift had been happy at the beginning at Moor Park he never intended to stay there for a long number of years. Sir William Temple knew many important people – even King William visited once to ask Temple's advice on some issue – and Swift always hoped that Temple would find a good job for him elsewhere. But as the years went by Temple came to rely more and more on Swift's help and so was not keen to lose him. Swift was very disappointed when he realised this. After nearly four years at Moor Park he wrote to his uncle William saying that, although Temple had made promises to him about a job, 'yet he is less forward than I could wish, because, I suppose, he believes I shall leave him and upon some accounts he thinks me a little necessary to him'.

CLERGYMAN AT KILROOT

In May 1694 Swift decided to leave Moor Park. He returned to Ireland to become a clergyman in the Church of Ireland. He was ordained in Christ Church Cathedral, Dublin, in January 1695. His life as a minister in the Church of Ireland did not turn out as he had hoped. He was sent to the parish of Kilroot near Belfast. The church at Kilroot was in a bad state of repair. Very few people came to his services as most of the people in the area were Presbyterians. While Swift's church was often empty, the Presbyterian meeting houses were full for their religious services.

The following story is told about his time in Kilroot: The situation there so annoyed Swift that one day he marched down to the shore with a wheelbarrow and filled it with stones. The people were curious to see what he was going to do with the stones and they followed him back to his church. Swift waited until the people were *inside* his church. Then he banged the doors shut and would not let them out until his service was over!

While in Kilroot Swift made friends with a young woman called Jane Waring. He fell in love with her and asked her to marry him. He was lonely and unhappy in Kilroot but he had decided to stay there if she would marry him. But Jane refused. Swift now decided there was no future for him in Kilroot. He returned to his old job as William Temple's assistant in Moor Park in the spring of 1696.

RETURN TO MOOR PARK

It must have been difficult for Swift to go back to Moor Park. He was a proud young man and ambitious too. When he had left Moor Park he hoped to make a career for himself in the church. Now he had to admit that things had not worked out as he had expected. Sir William Temple however was delighted to have him back. His wife had died while Swift was in Kilroot and he was lonely. Swift was lively, intelligent and witty. He loved jokes, games and good conversation and so he brought fresh life back with him to Moor Park.

Another person who was glad to see Swift return was Esther Johnson, or Stella, as Swift called her. She was now fifteen and growing into a beautiful young woman. Swift described her at the time as 'one of the most beautiful, graceful and agreeable young women in London, only a little too fat. Her hair was blacker than a raven and every feature of her face in perfection'. Swift and Stella now became very close friends. He enjoyed acting as her tutor, telling her what books to read, correcting her spelling, answering her questions and discussing things with her.

In those days young girls were not allowed to go out on their own; they had to have a companion with them. Stella's companion was an older woman called Rebecca Dingley. She was a cousin of William Temple's. She was not married but was known as 'Mrs' Dingley. Stella and Rebecca became lifelong friends.

Swift was hoping that Sir William Temple would arrange for him to be appointed vicar to a parish in London where he would have a large congregation and be in touch with the famous and important people of the day. But Temple was old now and in bad health, and he did nothing about obtaining such a position for Swift. Temple died in January 1699. Swift was now thirty-two and his hopes of obtaining a fine career through Temple's influence were finished. As he said later: 'Being born to no fortune, I was at his death as far to seek as ever.'

CHAPLAIN AT DUBLIN CASTLE

Swift had hoped to build a career for himself in England. After Temple's death, however, the only position he could find was as chaplain to the Earl of Berkeley who was going to Ireland as lord justice. (Ireland in those days was governed by a lord lieutenant who was always English or by three lords justice, two of whom were usually English.)

Having given up his hopes of a career in England for the time being, Swift sailed from England to Dublin with the Earl of Berkeley and his family in August 1699. Dublin Castle was then the centre of government in Ireland and so Swift moved into Dublin Castle with the Berkeley family. He was now living just a short distance from where he was born in Hoey's Court. He had hoped by this stage in his life to have been further away.

In spite of his disappointment, Swift enjoyed living in Dublin Castle. He got on well with the Berkeleys who were delighted to have such a lively companion staying with them. In those days when people had to make their own entertainment it was a great asset to have someone like Swift in the household. He loved word games and could make up amusing verses about people he met or incidents that occurred in the household.

In January 1700 the dean of Derry died. Swift hoped that he might be appointed to this important church position. He was disappointed again. Instead of Derry he was offered the much lower position of vicar of Laracor near Trim in Co. Meath. He accepted the position. It was at least better than his previous appointment in Kilroot. It was only fifteen miles, or half a day's horseback ride, from Dublin. This was important for Swift as he wanted to keep in touch with his friends in Dublin. There were only sixteen Protestant families in Laracor but this was considerably more than there had been in Kilroot. His income was also bigger. At Kilroot it had been £100 a year; now it was £230. This seems a tiny sum nowadays, but at that time it was quite a good income for a clergyman. We can realise the value of money then when we know that Swift's servant, who lived with him, received £4.50 a year in wages (his board and lodging of course were free). Another indication is that Swift in 1702 bought seven pairs of shoes for £1.50.

Swift still missed the larger world of London. So in April 1701 he set off for a six-month visit to England. He stayed with his mother in Leicester for a time and then went on to London. He spent the summer there.

Stella and Mrs Dingley were living in London now. Swift visited them often and discussed his life in Ireland with them. Swift suggested that, since Sir William and Lady Temple were now both dead and they had no real home, they should come and live in Ireland where he could meet them often. They were delighted with this suggestion and in August, having packed up their belongings, they sailed to Dublin.

Swift could not travel with them as he was due to accompany the new lord lieutenant to Ireland. He arrived in Dublin the following month on 17 September. There were gun salutes, cheering crowds and celebrations to welcome the new lord lieutenant but Swift was anxious to see how his dear friends had settled in so he slipped quietly away. He checked that they were comfortable in their new lodgings, and then went back to Laracor.

Swift spent most of the next six years in Ireland. In 1702 he took the degree of Doctor of Divinity at Trinity College. He was now known as Dr Swift.

When he had taken over as vicar of Laracor, the house and the land surrounding it were in a bad state of neglect. Swift now set about making improvements. He was a man of tremendous energy. Whenever he saw that things needed to be done he was never content to sit back and leave it to others. At Laracor he rebuilt the house and laid out an extensive garden. He cleaned and enlarged a river running through his property. He made a path alongside the river and planted double rows of willow trees, cherry trees and apple trees on the banks. Swift was very pleased with the results of his work and developed a strong affection for his home in the country. He wrote to a friend describing it: 'My river walk is extremely pretty and my canal in great beauty and I see trout playing in it.'

The sixteen Church of Ireland families in Laracor were, 'most of them gentle and all simple', according to Swift. The leading families in the parish were the Percivals, the Wesleys and the Langfords. He described them in the following rhyme:

> Mr Percival is ditching,
> Mrs Percival in her kitchen,
> Mr Wesley switching,
> Mrs Wesley stitching,
> Sir Arthur Langford riching.

Because of the small number of parishioners, sometimes there was no one at his services. At times like these, when only he and his church clerk Roger were there, instead of the traditional opening words of the prayers 'Dearly beloved brethren', he would begin with the words 'Dearly beloved Roger'.

When they first arrived in Dublin, Stella and Mrs Dingley had lodgings in William Street. This street is parallel to Grafton Street and is now a busy city-centre street. But in those days the main part of the city was around Dublin Castle, Christ Church Cathedral and the streets near the river, and William Street was little more than a country lane. One night an incident happened which made the women regret having chosen such an isolated spot to live in. Swift himself left us an account of the occurrence:

> Stella and her friend having removed their lodgings to a new house, which stood solitary, a parcel of rogues, armed, attempted the house, where there was only one boy. She was then about four-and-twenty; and having been warned to apprehend some such attempt, she learned the management of a pistol; and the other women and servants being half dead with fear, she stole softly to her dining-room window, put on a black hood to prevent being seen, primed the pistol fresh, gently lifted up the sash, and taking her

21

Stella defending her home against armed robbers.

aim with the utmost presence of mind, discharged the pistol loaded with the bullets into the body of one villain, who stood the fairest mark. The fellow was carried off by the rest.

After this event Stella and Mrs Dingley moved to a house near Capel Street which was a safer area as there were more people living there.

They went to visit Swift for long periods at Laracor. During these times they lived in a thatched cottage just down the road from the vicarage. This cottage was demolished in 1965. Part of the thatch and some of the original building materials from the house were saved and a model of the cottage was made with them. This model can be seen in the Heritage Centre in Trim.

Swift had a large circle of friends in Dublin and in the country. He spent a lot of time visiting them, staying for weeks, sometimes months. This was not unusual in those days when travel was difficult. Stella and Mrs Dingley often went with him on these visits.

Swift was very kind to his friends and spent a large amount of his income helping those in need. He used to give small loans to poor tradesmen in Trim to help them in their businesses. However, if he disapproved of someone, especially someone in a position of power, and if he felt they were doing wrong, he showed no mercy towards them. He would publish poems mocking them and exposing their faults. There was many a person who regretted getting on the wrong side of Dr Swift!

Swift was a man who held very strong views. He passionately hated dishonesty and hypocrisy. In 1704 he published a book called *A Tale of a Tub*. In this book he attacked hypocrisy in religion and among the clergy. The book was very successful and sold very well. Unfortunately some people thought he was attacking religion itself and this gave him a bad name.

MISSION TO LONDON

Although he loved his home at Laracor, Swift felt that his talents were wasted as a country vicar. But in 1707 an opportunity arose for him to play an important role in church affairs.

King William had died as a result of a fall from his horse in 1702 and Queen Anne was now on the throne in England. There was a tax on church income called the First Fruits tax which all clergymen had to pay to the State. In 1704 Queen Anne decided that the money from this tax in England should go to help poor clergymen. The bishops in the Church of Ireland wanted the same arrangement for the First Fruits money in Ireland. They asked Swift to go over to London to try to arrange this.

Swift was delighted with the opportunity to get involved in politics in London. He arrived there in November 1707. With his great talent for friendship he quickly made a lot of new friends. The closest of these new friends was a well known writer called John Addison who later started the newspaper *The Spectator*. Addison described Swift as 'the most agreeable companion, the truest friend and the greatest genius of the age'. Addison introduced Swift to another famous writer, Richard Steele, who edited the newspaper called *The Tatler*.

Swift used to meet his friends in the coffee houses in London. Coffee houses were then the

*Swift enjoyed many an evening's conversation in
coffee houses like this one.*

fashionable places for people to come together. They were really like clubs. There were coffee houses for artists, some where military men met, others for writers and politicians. If people felt like a chat they could call in to a particular coffee house where they would meet people with interests similar to their own. Swift liked to visit those where literary men met and he enjoyed joining in the conversations and discussions.

As usual Swift's life was full of activity. He enjoyed walking, riding, swimming and rowing. He loved reading and said: 'When I am reading a book, whether wise or silly, it seemeth to me to be alive and talking to me.' He wrote pamphlets – small printed papers that were sold on the streets for about a penny. In those days when there was no radio or television, people used pamphlets to get their ideas across to the public. He wrote articles for Steele's newspaper *The Tatler*, and one of his best known poems, 'A Description of the Morning', was written for the newspaper at this time.

All his life Swift loved playing jokes on people. One of the most famous jokes he played was on a fortune teller called John Partridge. In a series of pamphlets Swift pretended to be a fortune-teller named Bickerstaff. Under this name Swift foretold that Partridge would die on 29 March 1708. So many people believed this prediction that poor Partridge had a terrible time proving he was still alive! Although this joke was for fun there was a serious side to it too. Swift hated deception and dishonesty. He chose Partridge as a target for this joke because he knew Partridge was only deceiving people who paid him money to have their fortunes told.

Esther Vanhomrigh, whom Swift called Vanessa.

About this time Swift was out riding one day and called in to an inn for a cup of coffee. While sitting by the fire a young lady accidentally spilt his coffee over him. They began talking and quickly realised they had a lot in common. The young lady, whose name was Esther Vanhomrigh, was the daughter of a family who had been well known in Dublin. Her father had once been Dublin's Lord Mayor. He had died in 1703 and the family was now living in London. Esther, whom Swift nicknamed Vanessa, invited him to visit them. He accepted her offer and for the rest of his time in London he was a regular visitor to the house.

Vanessa was twenty-one years younger than Swift and he enjoyed acting as her tutor though, unlike Stella, she did not always follow his instructions. He described her this way:

> There is not a better girl on earth. I have a mighty friendship for her. She has good principles, and I have corrected her faults; but I cannot persuade her to read, though she has an understanding, memory and taste, that would bear great improvement. But she is incorrigibly idle and lazy – she thinks the world was made for nothing but perpetual pleasure.

Although he was enjoying his life in London, Swift was not having any success with his mission regarding the First Fruits tax money. He was constantly meeting politicians but they fobbed him off with promises that never came to anything. Realising he was getting nowhere, he decided in June 1709 to go back to Ireland. He paid a short visit to his mother and returned home dejected by his failure.

For the next four months Swift took up the threads of his life in Ireland. He spent a lot of time with Stella and travelled around the country renewing his friendships. He took up work again on his estate at Laracor, planting trees and making improvements. When visiting Dublin he had lodgings in Capel Street, close to Stella's house. His friend Addison was now at Dublin Castle as secretary to the lord lieutenant of the time. Addison often joined Swift, Stella and their friends for evenings of conversation and cardplaying.

THE ANTI-WAR CAMPAIGN

In 1710 different people were coming to power in the government in England and so Swift was sent back to London to try again to have the First Fruits tax money left with the Church of Ireland. The lord lieutenant was sailing back to England in August and Swift sailed with him.

Swift was delighted to be back in London. Invitations poured in from his friends to go and visit them. After a month in town he was able to write in a letter: 'It has cost me but three shillings in meat and drink since I came here.'

The new people in power in the English government were Robert Harley (who later became Earl of Oxford) and Henry St. John (later Lord Bolingbroke). Swift met Harley in October to discuss the First Fruits tax with him. The two men got on very well together. Within a month the Church of Ireland was granted permission to keep the First Fruits money on the same basis as the Church of England. Swift however never got the credit for this. When he had got agreement from the government about the tax, a different delegation from Dublin took over the negotiations and they got the credit. Swift was very hurt by this.

Although his First Fruits mission was now over, Swift's involvement in politics in London was only beginning. At this time England had been at war with France for nearly ten years. The English people were growing weary of this continuous warfare. The queen also wanted an end to the war. The previous year the leader of the English army, General Marlborough, had won a victory at the Battle of Malplaquat. This victory however had cost the lives of 18,000 of his men. The storm of protest against the war grew. Shortly afterwards Marlborough asked to be appointed Captain General of the army for life. The people were outraged at this request. A catchphrase, 'A General for life and our lives for the

General', could be heard in the streets whenever groups gathered to protest against the war.

The Whigs and the Tories were the two political parties in England at the time. The Whigs wanted the war to continue and the Tories wanted it to end. Harley was a Tory and wanted an end to warfare. Marlborough of course wanted the war to continue and he had a lot of Whig supporters. Harley now decided to run a campaign against Marlborough and the Whigs. He enlisted Swift's help in this campaign. He asked him to write and edit a newspaper called *The Examiner*. He wanted Swift to write articles supporting Tory policy and so bring about the downfall of Marlborough. Swift was delighted to do this. He hated war and the suffering it caused. He wrote:

War! That mad game the world so loves to play
And for it does so dearly pay.

Swift threw himself into the anti-war campaign with enthusiasm. He was now leading the kind of life he had always wanted. He was working at the source of power and was involved in the important decision-making of the day. Every evening he was invited out to dine and often afterwards would call into one of his favourite coffee houses to discuss the issues of the day with friends.

As well as his work on *The Examiner*, Swift wrote many pamphlets and poems at this time. He was now recognised in London as a brilliant writer. He became friendly with many of the other famous writers of the time. The closest of these friendships was with the poet Alexander Pope. They were to remain life-long friends.

In spite of all his activities he kept time every day

to write to Stella and Mrs Dingley. 'I must be writing every night. I cannot go to bed without a word to them. I can't put out my candle till I have bid them goodnight.' They were like a family for him and every evening when he came back to his room he enjoyed telling them all the happenings of his day.

Swift was now in lodgings at Bury Street, five doors down from the Vanhomrigh family. He described his rooms: 'I have the first floor, a dining room and a bedchamber at eight shillings a week.' He spent a lot of time with Vanessa and the Vanhomrighs. Theirs was an easy-going, hospitable household and he enjoyed relaxing there away from the affairs of state.

Harley's campaign against Marlborough, supported by Swift's pamphlets and articles in *The Examiner*, finally bore fruit in 1711. Marlborough was dismissed from his position in the army. The war itself finally came to an end when a peace treaty – the Treaty of Utrecht – was signed in 1713. Swift had played a large part in these events and now hoped to be rewarded with a good church position in England. Although vacancies occurred he was not appointed to any of them. It is thought that the bad name he had got for himself as author of *A Tale of a Tub* was the reason for this. Also the outspoken way in which he attacked people he disapproved of, many of them very important people, did not help his case. He believed this himself when he wrote:

Had he but spared his tongue and pen,
He might have rose like other men.

Eventually he was given an appointment – not in England as he had hoped, but in Ireland. In 1712 he received news that he was to be appointed dean

St Patrick's Cathedral, where Swift served as dean for thirty-two years.

of St Patrick's Cathedral in Dublin. He sailed for Ireland once more, arriving in Dublin in June 1713.

The parishioners of St Patrick's Cathedral were not too keen on the idea of having Swift as their dean. They had heard about his attacks on religion in *A Tale of a Tub*. When he arrived at the cathedral for his installation as dean the following lines were pinned to the doors:

> Look down St Patrick, look, we pray,
> On thine own church and steeple,
> Convert thy dean on this great day,
> or else God help the people.

The archbishop of Dublin at the time was a man called William King. When he heard Swift was to be the new dean he commented that it was good Swift had not been appointed a bishop because 'a dean can do less mischief than a bishop'.

Swift was very disappointed to find himself back in Ireland. He missed the bustle and excitement of his life in London. He wrote: 'I am condemned to live again in Ireland and all that the Court and Ministry did for me was to let me choose my station in the country where I am banished.'

He was not banished for long. Just three months after his installation in St Patrick's he returned to London where he remained for nearly a year. While there he published a political pamphlet *The Public Spirit of the Whigs* which so enraged the Scottish peers that the House of Lords condemned it as a malicious libel, and a price of £300 was put on Swift's head.

To add to his troubles he was now being watched

by the government authorities. Queen Anne had died in August 1714. The agreed successor to the throne of England was a German prince to be known as George I of England. Swift's friends, Lords Oxford and Bolingbroke, however, had got involved in negotiations to bring back James II's son as king of England. Therefore when George I took over they were found guilty of treason. Bolingbroke fled to France and Oxford was imprisoned in the Tower of London. Because of his friendship with them Swift now also fell under suspicion. His letters were opened and his movements watched. He was even hissed at in the streets of Dublin. This was all nonsense however because Swift would not have been at all in favour of James's son returning as king.

Swift kept in touch with his friends in England by writing long letters. In a letter to his friend Alexander Pope he described his life in Ireland:

> You are to understand that I live in the corner of a vast unfurnished house; my family consists of a steward, a groom, a helper in the stable, a foot-man, and an old maid ... and when I do not dine abroad ... I eat a mutton-pye, and drink half a pint of wine. My amusements are defending my small dominions against the archbishop, and endeavouring to reduce my rebellious choir.

As well as being dean of St Patrick's he was still vicar of Laracor. He liked to escape from the gloomy deanery to his house at Laracor. Stella and Mrs Dingley often went with him.

One day while he was riding on the road outside Trim, a messenger caught up with him and handed him a letter. He was surprised to find that it was a note from Vanessa. She had followed him to Ireland and was now living in a house her family owned at Celbridge, Co. Kildare. In the letter she asked him to come and visit her. Swift was not too pleased with the news. When their friendship had begun seven years earlier Swift had wanted them to be friends, with him acting as her advisor. As the years went by, however, Vanessa fell hopelessly in love with Swift. He did not return her love. In a poem he wrote for her at that time he explained:

> But time and books and state affairs
> Had spoiled his fashionable airs;
> He now could praise, esteem, approve,
> But understood not what was love.

Swift now sent a message back saying he could not visit her at Celbridge but would see her in Dublin. She had taken lodgings at a place called Turnstile Alley, near Trinity College, where she could stay when in town.

On arrival back in Dublin Swift visited Vanessa and tried to explain that he would not be able to call often. Poor Vanessa was very lonely and unhappy. Her mother had died before she came to Ireland and now she was alone with her sister in a country where she knew hardly anyone. She kept begging Swift to come and see her again. Swift enjoyed her company and visited her regularly but did not want to become too deeply involved with her. He advised her to get out more and meet people, but she was not interested. She was happy only when Swift visited her. She marked each of his visits to Celbridge by planting a laurel.

Swift helping the poor of Dublin.

In his first years as dean of St Patrick's, Swift hated the poverty and backwardness of Ireland. In letters to his friends he called it 'this miserable country'. He tried to help the poor people living around the cathedral in the Liberties by lending them money to help them buy tools and other things they needed to start up a business. He also gave away a lot of money to beggars who congregated around the cathedral. Then after some years his attitude changed. Instead of just being annoyed at having to live in a country where there was so much misery and poverty, he began to ask himself why the people were in such a wretched condition. He came to the conclusion that the main reason was the way the English governed Ireland.

In Swift's time most of the people living around St Patrick's Cathedral were weavers. They made woollen material mainly, but also silk and linen. They were very poor. They found it hard to sell the cloth they produced. The main reason for this was that the English government has passed a law prohibiting the weavers from exporting their cloth and selling it abroad. Therefore they could only sell in Ireland. There were problems here too because many of the well-off people in Ireland preferred to buy English cloth and so the weavers sank deeper and deeper into poverty. Archbishop King described the situation:

> The poverty of the kingdom is not to be imagined. The cry of the weavers of all sorts, linen, woollen and silk, was intolerable. They sold and pawned all they had for bread – household stuff, clothes, looms and tools, and there remained nothing behind but to starve.

They prepared a petition to the government and council, who offered them £100 and a collection in the church. The numbers of the weaving trade are near 1,700, and the persons near 6,000. What will come of them God only knows. It is true everybody bestirred themselves to get them a supply, the Dissenters, the Roman Catholics, the Deans and Chapters, the College, nay the Playhouse gave a play which raised £73. So that we have got a fund which, I hope, will amount to near £1,500. But what will this be among so many?

In 1714, shortly after taking up his appointment as dean of St Patrick's, Swift wrote: 'I hope I shall keep my resolution of never meddling with Irish politics.' Now, six years later, in 1720, he was so angered by the condition of the people around him that he decided he would have to get involved in politics again. He would have to speak on behalf of the poor who could not speak for themselves.

As a result of this decision Swift wrote a pamphlet called *A Proposal for the Universal Use of Irish manufacture in Clothes and Furniture of Houses, etc, utterly Rejecting and Renouncing Everything Wearable that comes from England.* In this pamphlet he attacked the English laws that caused the poverty of the weavers in the city. He also attacked the landlords in the country who, he wrote, by 'racking their tenants all over the kingdom have already reduced the miserable people to a worse condition than the peasants in France or the vassals in Germany and Poland'.

As a solution to the problems of the weavers and other producers of goods, Swift suggested that people in Ireland should buy only Irish products.

He was therefore the very first person to put forward the idea of a 'Buy Irish' campaign. He suggested that people should burn everything English except their coal! Swift's pamphlet was enormously popular and sold by the thousand. His ideas became the talk of the town. The weavers in the parish now looked on him as a hero.

The representatives of the English government in Dublin however were furious with Swift. They could not take any action against the dean himself, because he had not put his name to the pamphlet, but they arrested the printer and brought him to trial. He was accused of printing a false and dangerous document. The jury at his trial however refused to find the printer guilty. The judge sent them back eight times to reconsider their verdict but they still refused to find him guilty. In the end the case was dropped. This result was hailed as a great victory by Swift's supporters and he became more popular than ever.

HOPE DIES FOR VANESSA

Vanessa continued her lonely life at Celbridge. She wrote many pleading letters to Swift: 'Is it possible you will come and see me? I beg for God's sake you will. I would give the world to see you here!' He continued to visit her occasionally but this was not enough. She wrote: 'Tis now ten long, long weeks since I saw you and in all that time I have never received but one letter from you.'

Because of Swift's close friendship with Stella rumours were flying around Dublin that Swift and Stella had been secretly married. Eventually Vanessa heard these rumours. Very distressed, she wrote to Stella asking if it was true. When Swift heard about this he was very angry. He did not want Vanessa upsetting Stella. In a fury he rode out to Celbridge and stormed into the house. He flung the letter down on the table in front of Vanessa. Then, saying he never wanted to see her again, he turned on his heel and left. This was the end of the road for Vanessa. She now had no hope of happiness left. She died soon afterwards of a broken heart.

WOOD'S HALFPENCE

Following the death of Vanessa, Swift left Dublin for a long sojourn in the country. For several months he wandered around the south of Ireland. He travelled on horseback, and was away for several months. During this time a great controversy arose in Dublin over the minting of small Irish coins.

In Ireland in the early 1700s there was a shortage of copper coins – halfpence and farthings. A worker's wage at the time was between 6 pence and 12 pence a week, and most of the transactions of the poor, the vast majority of the population, would have been carried out in copper coinage.

In 1722 a patent to mint new money was granted by the Crown to the Duchess of Kendal. She sold the patent to an English manufacturer called William Wood for £10,000, an enormous sum of money in those days. The patent allowed Wood to mint £100,800 worth of copper coins. Wood stood to make a vast profit for himself and swamp Ireland with copper money.

The Irish parliament had not been consulted on the matter and decided to resist the patent and it was generally agreed that only £10,000 to £20,000 in copper was needed to cover the shortage. After meeting to discuss the matter, parliament warned the government in London that anything over this amount would not be accepted in Ireland.

Wood was so sure that no one could interfere with the king's patent that he began minting the money in the summer of 1723. When he heard there was opposition to the patent he boasted openly that he would force his coinage on the Irish.

DRAPIER'S LETTERS

On his return to Dublin in January 1724 Swift learned that the opposition to Wood's patent had grown. Despite the warnings from both houses of parliament in Dublin the patent was not withdrawn. Swift regarded Ireland as an independent kingdom, and not a colony, and he was furious that the wishes of the Irish parliament were ignored. He saw the patent as further exploitation of an already sorely oppressed country by her more powerful neighbour. He decided that the time had come to take a firm stand.

In February 1724 he wrote the first of the four famous *Drapier's Letters*. These were pamphlets protesting against Wood's coins. Swift asked the printer Mr Harding to sell the pamphlet at the lowest rate to ensure that as many people as possible could buy it. As everyone in the land was affected by the new coinage Swift intended to unite the whole country in a mass protest against the scheme. For Swift the whole country meant the Irish Protestants, from tradesman to nobleman. He detested the Dissenters and though he disliked and mistrusted the Catholics he was sympathetic to their plight.

Swift wrote the letters under the name of M.B. Drapier, a fictitious shopkeeper from Francis

Street, but everyone in Dublin knew who the author was. The first letter was addressed *To The Shopkeepers, Tradesmen, Farmers and Common People of Ireland*. In it Drapier advises them not to accept Mr Wood's coins in payment, as they are worthless. He says they are of such poor quality that they will be easily counterfeited by others and the country will be flooded with coins of little value. He assures the people that to make even the smallest transaction they will need ten times as many halfpence as before.

Drapier has great fun exaggerating the situation, claiming that if a squire comes to town to buy provisions for his family, 'he must bring with him five or six horses well laden with sacks of copper coin to pay his bill'. And if a lady comes to shop then her coach would have to be followed 'by a car loaded with Mr Wood's money'. He warns that they are being cheated by Wood and pleads: 'Therefore, my friends, stand to it one and all, refuse this filthy trash.'

Robert Walpole, the English prime minister, was alarmed by all the opposition and an order was issued restricting the amount of Wood's coinage to £40,000. It was rumoured at the time that Wood's coins would have more brass and less copper than similar English coins and would therefore be less valuable. To allay fear, some of the coins were sent to be assayed – tested for their quality – by Sir Isaac Newton, the famous scientist. Newton, who was then the Master of the Mint at the Tower of London, found the coins to be of perfectly good quality.

But the furore would not die down and on 4 August Drapier wrote a second letter. In it he suggested that Wood had tried to deceive everyone

Dubliners burn an effigy of Wood in a demonstration against Wood's halfpence.

by taking 'care to coin a dozen or two halfpence of good metal', and that these special coins were the ones sent to Newton for analysis. But, Drapier assured his readers, nobody in Ireland would be fooled by this deliberate ruse.

Walpole's concession to reduce the amount of the patent meant that the resistance was having the desired effect, so Swift fired off the third Drapier letter *To the Nobility and Gentry of the Kingdom of Ireland*. These were the people who sat in the Irish parliament. In this letter he cleverly pointed out the threat to the nation's independence by posing questions that would strike home: 'Were not the people of Ireland born as free as those in England? Am I a freeman in England and do I become a slave in six hours by crossing the Channel?'

Swift knew very well that the Irish parliament held little power since the Declaratory Act of 1719. This Act gave the British parliament the right to make laws 'to bind the kingdom and people of Ireland'. Nevertheless he goaded the nobles to act, not against the king, which would have been treason, but against Wood, stressing that there was no law saying anyone had to accept the coins.

Shortly after this letter appeared the anti-Wood campaign reached new heights. At a big demonstration in Dublin an effigy of Wood was paraded through the streets and burned. People flocked to sign petitions against the halfpence. Anti-Wood poems and doggerels appeared, much to the delight of Swift. He had finally stirred the Irish into action and roused their national pride.

There was action in London too. Walpole decided to send over a new lord lieutenant, Lord John Carteret, to Dublin as he did not like the defiant attitude of the Irish. Swift got wind of the appointment and before Carteret set foot in Ireland the fourth Drapier letter was on the streets. This letter *To the Whole People of Ireland* claims that many of the Englishmen holding high offices in Ireland had obtained their positions by corrupt means. Drapier questions the right of the lord lieutenant 'to impose Wood's halfpence on the people of Ireland', stating that 'government without the consent of the governed is the very definition of slavery.' Swift described the English lord lieutenant's task in Ireland as follows:-

And what condition can be worse?
He comes to drain a Beggar's Purse:
He comes to tye our Chains on faster,
And show us England is our Master.

THE HIBERNIAN PATRIOT

When Lord Carteret read the fourth Drapier letter he considered it to be treasonable. He ordered the arrest of the printer Harding, and offered a reward of £300 for the discovery of the author. But though every man, woman and child in Dublin knew who had written the letters, no one claimed the reward. This was the second time a £300 reward was put on his head, and Swift, delighted, wrote:

And not a traitor could be found,
To sell him for six hundred pound.

The reward in fact had just the opposite effect. It united the people behind Swift and his praises were sung in the streets. There was no stopping him now. Before Harding's trial Swift wrote a pamphlet to the Grand Jury advising them that as Dr King, the archbishop of Dublin had refused to condemn the book or the author he was sure they would do likewise. At Harding's trial on 21 November 1724 the jury, when called on by Lord Chief Justice Whitshed to give their verdict, refused to convict the printer. Whitshed dismissed them and brought in a new jury. They too refused to convict and instead, inspired by Swift, delivered a statement against 'all persons who had attempted to impose Wood's halfpence upon us.' Harding was released. This gave Swift great satisfaction and he told a friend: 'The government and the judges are at their wits' end.'

Whitshed's behaviour at the trial made him Swift's next target. One day Swift's sharp eye had noticed the motto on the side of the judge's coach: 'Libertas et natale solum' (Liberty and my native country). As Whitshed was one of the few Irish to hold high office, we can easily imagine Swift chuckling to himself as he made up the following lampoon:

Libertas et natale solum,
Fine words: I wonder where you stole 'um.
Libertas bears a large import;
First, how to swagger in a court;
And secondly, to show my fury,
Against an uncomplying jury.
And thirdly, 'tis a new invention,
To favour Wood and keep my pension ...

The British government eventually acted and in 1725 Wood's patent was withdrawn. *The Drapier Letters* had made Swift a national hero and he became known throughout Ireland as 'The Hibernian Patriot.' Despite the hullabaloo over Wood's halfpence, Lord Carteret remained on good terms with Swift. Though he must have known that he

The figure of Gulliver, made for the Dublin millennium celebrations, 1988, seen here on Dollymount Strand.

was the author of the *Drapier's Letters*, he continued to invite him to Dublin Castle. Years later when asked how he managed to govern in Ireland Carteret replied: 'I pleased Dr Swift.'

GULLIVER'S TRAVELS

The *Drapier's Letters* were written during a very busy and happy period in Swift's life. As well as attacking Wood's halfpence he was also writing what was to become his most famous work, *Gulliver's Travels*. The original idea for the *Travels* had come from the Scriblerus Club. This literary club had been set up by Swift and his friends in the spring of 1714 in London where they met regularly to discuss both serious and trivial matters and to enjoy one another's company. The members, who included Pope, Addison and Bolingbroke, were to write a book as a joint venture but nothing ever came of it, though the idea remained in Swift's mind. In the early eighteenth century stories of exploration in new and strange lands and long sea voyages were capturing the public's imagination. Daniel Defoe's *Robinson Crusoe* was published in 1719 and enjoyed great success. These stories may have influenced Swift in his choice of a light-hearted travel tale in which to hide some serious criticism of his fellow men.

Swift wrote part of his famous story while staying with his friend Tom Sheridan at Quilca in County Cavan. Nearby lived a farmer called 'Big Doughty', who was famous in the county for his great height and incredible strength. There is a local tradition that he showed off his prowess to the visiting dean by carrying a horse from one field to another across a stile. Swift who loved anything eccentric was delighted by this huge feat of strength and is said to have based his hero Gulliver, the giant, on 'Big Doughty'.

He started writing the book in 1721 and four years later wrote to his friend Ford: 'I have just finished my *Travels* and am now transcribing them. They are admirable things and will wonderfully mend the world.' Early in 1726 Swift packed the manuscript and went to London to find a publisher and spend a few months with his old friends. In August he wrote to Benjamin Motte, a London printer, offering for sale the travels of his cousin Mr Lemuel Gulliver. As he did not want his identity to be known he signed the letter Richard Sympson. Motte later told Pope that the manuscript of *Gulliver's Travels* was 'dropped at his house in the dark from a hackney coach', in great secrecy.

On his return to Dublin, Swift was given a great welcome: 'Leading citizens met his ship in wherries festooned with colours and streamers; church bells were rung and bonfires lit.'

The first edition of *Gulliver's Travels* was published on 28 October 1726. It was a sell-out and had to be reprinted twice that year. Two further editions were printed in 1727. The book has remained popular ever since. It is Swift's most famous work and is still read and enjoyed all over the world by both adults and children. Although the book has a serious side, it is as a children's classic that it is best loved.

LILLIPUT

Lemuel Gulliver's first adventure starts when he is shipwrecked in a terrible storm. After a long struggle in raging seas he eventually reaches land

Gulliver in the Land of Lilliput.

where, exhausted, he falls asleep. When he awakes he finds to his horror that he is tied up from head to toe and surrounded by hundreds of little people, 'not six inches high', armed with bows and arrows. These are the Lilliputians. They are terrified of the great giant who has landed in their country.

Still bound, and after much difficulty, Gulliver is placed on a hastily-made carriage and drawn by 1500 horses, not 4 inches high, to the emperor's palace. The emperor orders a search to be made of Gulliver's pockets and every child loves the list of things found in them: one great piece of coarse cloth (a handkerchief); a huge silver chest which was full of dust that made everyone sneeze a lot (a snuff box); a bundle of white thin substances, folded one over the other about the bigness of three men, tied with strong cable marked with black figures (a note book with writing on it); a sort of engine with twenty long poles (a comb); a hollow pillar of iron fastened to a strong piece of timber (a pistol). In a small pocket were found several pieces of white and red metal (some silver and copper money), and on a great silver chain was an engine with strange figures circularly drawn which made incessant noise like that of a waterfall (a pocket watch).

Gulliver's Travels is full of humour, satire and adventures. There is great fun in the difficulties that beset the Lilliputians with the arrival of a giant in their midst. They have to work out how much food he will need to eat. Ladders have to be used to measure him for clothes, and no less than six hundred beds have to be sewn together to make a bed for Gulliver.

There is humour in the make up of the squabbling parties that govern in Lilliput – the high heels and the low heels. The emperor belonged to the low heels but his son and heir was inclined to the high heels and so wore one heel higher than the other. This made him a funny sight, as the hobbled when he walked.

We find satire when Gulliver learns the reason why Lilliput is at war with her nearest neighbour Blefuscu for 'six and thirty moons past'. The war arose over which end of an egg should be broken before eating it – the larger end or the smaller end. The folly of going to war for such a petty reason greatly puzzled Gulliver. Swift used this story to illustrate his own horror of war.

When the emperor seeks Gulliver's help to prevent an invasion by the Blefuscu fleet an exciting adventure ensues. In a daring raid the giant seizes the enemy fleet with both hands and tows it back to Lilliput where for his bravery he is awarded the highest honour in the land by the emperor. However, things turn sour when Gulliver refuses to assist the emperor in his scheme to take over the whole country of Blefuscu. For this refusal the ruling council brand him a traitor and decide to punish him by the loss of his eyes. Fortunately Gulliver has a good friend on the council who warns him of the impending danger. Poor Gulliver is perplexed by the fact that a country he had just saved from an enemy invasion now wishes to harm him. He escapes from Lilliput before they can carry out the punishment.

A VOYAGE TO BROBDINGNAG

On his second voyage Gulliver, through no fault of his own, is left behind on the island of Brobdingnag. This place is just as strange as Lilliput but for

Gulliver in Brobdingnag.

the opposite reason – it is a land of giants. Again the story has elements of humour, adventure and wit.

The fun begins when Gulliver encounters the local giants for the first time. He is so terrified by their huge size (they are as tall as church steeples), that he hides out in a hayfield. There he is discovered by a farmer who is not quite sure whether he has found an animal or an insect. To show the giant that he too is a man, though of a very different size, Gulliver marches up and down, bows and scrapes, doffs his hat in salute and shouts at the top of his voice. The farmer is fascinated by these antics and takes him home to show him to the family.

Gulliver, placed on the kitchen table, is astonished by the enormity of everything he sees. The cat looks three times bigger than an ox. Gulliver is frightened out of his wits by the family dogs who seem to him the size of four elephants. The farmer's baby thinks he is a toy and stuffs him in its mouth and the farmer's wife screams because she thinks he is some kind of spider. Gulliver wonders will he survive long among such dangers. The farmer puts him on show in the towns and cities and he is nearly worked to death performing endless tricks for the crowds who flock to see him. Then he is sold to the Queen of Brobdingnag.

At court things get worse for him. He is nearly knocked out by hailstones the size of tennis balls. He is attacked by giant wasps, grabbed and left on a rooftop by an enormous monkey and breaks a leg falling over a huge snail in the palace gardens. While showing off his sailing skills to the queen his toy boat is knocked over by a large frog. These mishaps keep everyone at court amused except, of course, Gulliver.

To make up for his insignificant size he boasts to the King of Brobdingnag about his country, England, its great rulers and how they came to power. He gets a shock when the king forms the opinion that to obtain a position of power in England one has to be ignorant, idle and corrupt! The king 'gave it for his opinion that whoever could make two blades of corn or two blades of grass to grow where only one had grown before would deserve better of mankind and do more essential service to his country than the whole race of politicians put together.' This is Swift's way of attacking those in power in England who were more interested in politics and commerce than in improving the condition of the land and the people.

Gulliver is even more surprised when the monarch rebuffs his offer to give him the secret of gunpowder. The king, on learning that it could be used to dash out people's brains, sink ships and batter cities to the ground, is horrified that such an inhuman invention could exist. He forbids Gulliver, on peril of his life, ever to mention the subject again in his kingdom.

Fortunately for Gulliver, before he can get into more trouble, he is snatched up by a large bird of prey, dropped in the ocean and rescued by a passing ship bound for England.

LAPUTA

In the seventeenth and eighteenth centuries science was gaining a hold on popular imagination. The Royal Society in London was the major scientific institute at the time. Scientists, or projectors as they were then called, were carrying out research in mathematics, astrology, flying machines, chemistry, physics and language. Living in Dublin during Swift's lifetime was a man called Richard Pockrich. Pockrich was an inventor who had schemes for flying machines, new musical instruments, blood transfusions and iron boats. Although laughed at by his contemporaries, many of his ideas have since come to pass. Swift would have been familiar with all that was going on in the scientific world and he disliked what he saw. He set Gulliver's third voyage in a land governed by scientific theory in order to mock the new scientists and show what can happen when man abandons reason.

After quite an adventure Gulliver arrives in Laputa, a fantastic flying island. The people there are the strangest Gulliver has ever met. They are interested only in music, astrology and mathematics and are incapable of doing anything practical. He visits their 'Academy' which is full of projectors carrying out crackpot experiments. One is trying to make ice into gunpowder, another has been eight years trying to extract sunbeams out of cucumbers. An architect is working on a new method of building houses by starting at the roof and working downwards. In the School of Mathematics the pupils are experimenting with a new learning technique. The professor explains to Gulliver that they swallow the texts on a thin wafer and after three days, if his theory works, the answers will be absorbed by their brains. Needless to say he was experiencing some difficulties. The Language School is working on a scheme to make language easy by abolishing all words! At the School of Political Science the professors are trying to develop a system which if successful would end party disputes; the idea being that a hundred men from each party, with similar sized heads, would have half their brains transplanted into the heads of their opposite numbers. As each would then think alike there would be no further disputes. Gulliver is bewildered by all the hare-brained experiments and returns home at the first opportunity.

Gulliver's Travels added two new words to our vocabulary, Lilliputian and Yahoo. Swift sent Gulliver on a fourth voyage, seldom included in children's versions of the book, where he met the Yahoos. The word is still used to day to mean a brutish or boorish person.

Jonathan Swift described his book to a friend as a 'merry work' and as you can see it is full of comic incidents. But Swift cleverly used comedy both to entertain and to mock and this is why the book is enjoyed 'from the cabinet to the nursery.'

When the book was published in London it caused quite a stir. It was the talk of the town. Several people claimed they knew Lemuel Gulliver. Others searched their maps to locate the strange lands Gulliver had visited, believing them to be real places. An Irish bishop thinking it was meant to be a true story said it was full of lies. These responses to the book must have greatly amused Swift. By 1728 Gulliver's Travels had been translated into French, German and Dutch and was being read throughout Europe. In Dublin, people snapped up every copy that arrived in the bookshops and there was much talk of Yahoos and Lilliputians.

STELLA'S DEATH

In April 1727 Swift left Stella and Mrs Dingley at

the deanery and went to England to spend the summer with his old friends. It was to be his farewell visit. He never again returned to England. His friends Pope and Bolingbroke were delighted to see him and he enjoyed being the centre of attention.

Towards the end of August his closest friend in Ireland, Tom Sheridan, wrote that Stella was very ill and dying. Swift set out for Ireland but was stranded for a week at Holyhead because of bad weather. He was very annoyed at the delay and wrote crustily:

Lo here I sit at holy head
With muddy ale and mouldy bread
All christian vittals s tink of fish
I'm where my enemies would wish ...

Stella was still alive when Swift reached Dublin. She lingered on for a few months and died on 28 January 1728. Swift was dining at the deanery when he heard 'of the death of the truest, most virtuous and valuable friend that I, or perhaps any other person, ever was blessed with'. The following evening Stella was buried in St Patrick's Cathedral. Swift did not go to her funeral. He wrote in his diary: 'My sickness will not suffer me to attend.' The night she died he wrote a loving account of her, praising her modesty, beauty and intelligence. He also paid tribute to her charity and good sense and her love of Ireland: 'She loved Ireland better than the generality of those who owe both their birth and riches to it.' Stella left her small fortune to Dr Steeven's Hospital which continued to serve the people of Dublin until it was closed in 1987.

*A contemporary picture by Hogarth of a sleeping congregation.
Swift was very critical of bad preachers like this one and
gave advice on how to keep the congregation awake!*

After Stella's death Swift's Irish friends were extremely kind to him. He was often invited by Lord and Lady Howth to dine at Howth Castle. Sheridan kept in constant touch, and Lord and Lady Acheson had him to stay with them at Market Hill near Armagh for over six months. This visit was so long that Swift, always able to laugh at himself, suggested in a poem that Lady Acheson was probably saying the following about him to her husband:

> The house accounts are daily rising,
> So much his stay does swell the bills,
> My dearest life it is surprising,
> How much he eats, how much he swills.

Back in Dublin after his extended visit to Market Hill he threw himself once more into his daily routine. He was a non-stop worker. Besides his writings he was kept busy at the cathedral where he was an outstanding dean. On his appointment he found both church and church services had been badly neglected. Despite opposition from some of his clergy and congregation, he restored the weekly Communion Service and set about repairing the cathedral buildings. He preached regularly in St Patrick's and is known to have exhorted his flock to stay awake and listen lest while snoozing they fall off their seats and injure themselves!

Swift had very definite ideas about how to write a good sermon. We can read his ideas on this subject in a letter he wrote to a young clergyman. He advises him to use plain, simple words that can be understood by everyone in the congregation and he complains about the habit clergymen, lawyers and professors have of using difficult words and ideas that no-one can understand just to make themselves seem important. 'Proper words in proper places,' he says, 'makes the true definition of a style.'

As dean he also took a great interest in the cathedral choir and insisted that only the best singers were given places. When Lady Carteret, the lord lieutenant's wife, wanted a place in the choir for a friend he refused, saying: 'If your friend wanted a bishopric I might consider your request as that position requires no special talent, but a member of a choir must be able to sing.' Handel, the great composer, is said to have called at the deanery to seek permission for the choir to sing his oratorio *The Messiah* which was being performed for the first time in nearby Fishamble Street.

Swift also looked after the monuments in the cathedral, and on learning that the Duke of Schomberg, who was killed during the Battle of the Boyne, was buried there, he wrote to the duke's family in Holland requesting money to erect a suitable memorial. When they refused his request he went ahead anyway and wrote the following inscription on the black marble tablet: 'The renown of his valour was more appreciated among strangers than among his own kith and kin.' This memorial can be seen in the north choir aisle in the cathedral. A similar story is told of the Boyle monument in the west end of the nave, but the Boyle family, fearing they might be publicly ridiculed, did not dare cross the dean and sent on the necessary funds.

Swift also found time for one of his favourite pastimes – gardening. He bought a plot of land, which must have been a graveyard, and he cleared away the headstones to one side and planted fruit trees. This garden, known as Swift's 'cabbage garden', with the old headstones resting against the wall and still planted with cherry trees, is situated at the top of Cathedral Lane opposite the deanery.

Throughout his lifetime, Swift was known for charitable deeds. He was a popular figure in the Liberties as his pockets were always full of small change for the poor. It is easy to imagine the portly dean striding along the narrow streets near the cathedral, digging deep into his pockets for something to offer the ever-present beggars. Not everyone received his help, however. He is said to have shouted to one old beggarwoman, who put out a filthy hand for a coin: 'Nothing for you while your hands are dirty, even beggars can wash.' Apart from giving a third of his income to the poor, Swift started an almshouse for widows and a school for local children. When a woman he knew was in need, Swift sent her a plum cake with a note saying he hoped she liked plums. She was puzzled until she started to eat the cake and discovered that the 'plums' were guineas wrapped in paper.

Above all, Swift continued to write about the problems affecting the people of Ireland. Between 1727 and 1729 the country was hit by famine. In August 1729 Swift wrote to Pope: 'There have been three terrible years' dearth of corn and every place is strewed with beggars.' Times were very bad. Thousands perished or emigrated during these wretched years. Swift began to despair that no one in either Ireland or England would heed his warnings on the state of the country. For ten years he had been publishing pamphlets urging the Irish to help themselves and the English overlords to ease the intolerable trade embargos which were ruining the Irish economy. His warnings went unheard and now with the onset of famine all he could see about him was awful poverty and destitution.

In October 1729 Swift published an angry and bitter attack on the administration, known as *A Modest Proposal*. In this pamphlet he set out to shock and, if possible, goad the authorities into action by suggesting that poor children should be cooked and eaten as a way of solving their appalling plight! He did not mean his outrageous suggestion to be taken literally, he simply used the most horrific idea he could think of to arouse sympathy and attention for the miserable people. The absentee and money-grabbing landlords were attacked for their greed and neglect and the authorities in both countries for ignoring his earlier pleas for action. He rebuked the landlords with biting sarcasm: 'I grant this food will be somewhat dear and therefore very proper for landlords, who, as they have already devoured most of the parents, seem to have best title to the children.' *A Modest Proposal* was to be Swift's greatest outburst on behalf of the destitute in Ireland.

MORE HUMOUR AND VERSE

As he grew older Swift's deafness and giddiness increased but he remained active, continuing his work at the cathedral, his endless correspondence and his writings. Though often depressed and weary from his illness, his good humour never deserted him. When he heard that Bishop Rundle of Derry had fallen from his horse he could not resist remarking:

*Bettesworth, armed with a knife, came to threaten Swift,
who had mocked him in a poem.*

Friend Rundle fell with grievous bump,
Upon his reverential rump.

He could also laugh at himself and his illness:

The old vertigo in his head,
Will never leave him till he's dead,
Besides his memory decays,
He recollects not what he says ...

He wrote a poem mocking a Mr Bettesworth who deeply resented the attack and threatened to cut off his ears. Bettesworth, armed with a sharp knife, arrived at the deanery to carry out his threat, but the people in the Liberties frightened him off. They had made a pact among themselves to defend Swift against any such attacks. For this affront Bettesworth was further ridiculed and sung about in the streets in this refrain:

Jolly boys of St Kevin's, St Patrick's, Donore,
And Smithfield, I'll tell, if not told before,
How Bettesworth, that booby, and scoundrel in grain,
Hath insulted us all by insulting the Dean.

The following lines attacking Walpole, the English prime minister, and King George II, caused the arrest of the London publisher Gilliver, and Swift was lucky to escape the same fate.

Should a monkey wear a crown,
Must I tremble at his frown?
Could I not, through all his ermine
Spy the strutting, chattering vermin?

Walpole was so incensed that he wanted to have Swift arrested, but was warned by Lord Carteret that it would take an army of ten thousand men to remove Swift from the deanery. The prime minister wisely desisted.

Although honoured and revered by the people of Dublin since the *Drapier's Letters*, it was not until 1730, six years later, that Swift was given the freedom of the city. He has left an amusing account of the day and what he said to the lord mayor and aldermen who came to the deanery to present him with his scroll of freedom in a gold box. He said he was much obliged to his Lordship and the city for the honour they were going to do him, and which, as he was informed, they had long intended him. That it was true this honour was mingled with a little mortification by the delay which attended it. He suggested that the gold box, which was plain, might be engraved to mark the occasion. And he told the delegation that he was indeed the author of the *Drapier's Letters*. This was the first time he admitted it publicly. In 1736 the Corporation of Cork granted him the freedom of their city. This same year his birthday was celebrated publicly in Dublin with a gun salute and in verse.

This year also saw Swift's last intervention in Irish politics. It was an attack on the landlords in parliament who wanted to abolish the tithe on pasture. Swift hated the lazy, self-centered parliamentarians who did nothing for the country, and he lampooned them for posterity in 'The Legion Club'.

As I strole the City, oft I
Spy a building large and lofty,
Not a bow-shot from the College,

Half the globe from sense and knowledge.
Tell us what this pile contains,
Many a head that holds no brains.

The 'large building' was the house of parliament which in Swift's time was in College Green, opposite Trinity College.

Swift by now had become a hero to the ordinary people in Ireland. Bishop Nicholson once described him as 'the darling of the populace'. The people were delighted to hear an important voice raised on their behalf against the politicians and landlords and they grew to love this eccentric clergyman who was the first person to plead their genuine grievances.

Tom Sheridan said that 'Swift was known over the whole kingdom by the title of "The Dean" and when "The Dean" was mentioned it always carried with it the idea of the first and the greatest man in the kingdom – whatever he said or did was received as infallibly right'. This is borne out by the story of an incident which took place outside the deanery. One evening Swift was disturbed from his writing by a large rowdy crowd gathered beneath his window to watch an eclipse of the sun. Annoyed by the noise they were making, he threw open his window and declared that the eclipse had been postponed and they could all go home! The crowd believed him and quietly dispersed.

On another occasion when a proclamation was issued to devalue the Irish guinea, Swift fought vigorously to have it withdrawn. When the devaluation went ahead, the dean had a black flag hoisted from the top of St Patrick's and ordered the bell ringers to toll a funeral peal all day long as a mark of protest. Swift was such a strong personality that many stories were told about him throughout the country. There is a whole collection of tales in Irish folklore about the dean and his servant Jack, the most famous of which is 'the leg of the goose'. In the story the servant, who is given little to eat, devours one leg of the roast goose before he serves it at table. The dean angrily demands to know what happened to the other leg and is told by Jack that geese have only one leg. Later in the day when the dean and Jack are out riding Jack points to a flock of geese standing in a pond on one leg. The dean claps his hands and shouts 'Whoosh' and of course the geese put down their other leg. 'Now, you scoundrel,' shouts Swift, 'they have two legs!' 'But sir,' says Jack, 'why didn't you do that with the goose I laid before you at dinner!'

Tradition also connects Swift with the blind harper Turlough O'Carolan. Several of his friends were patrons of Carolan and it is known that the harper composed the music for Hugh MacGauran's poem 'Pléaraca na Ruarcach' – a description of an Irish feast which Swift translated into English. The song records a great feast held by O'Rourke, Prince of Breifne, who was later hanged at Tyburn for helping the Spanish survivors from the famous Armada.

This is part of Swift's translation:

O'Rourke's noble Fare,
Will ne'er be forgot,
By those who were there,
or those who were not.
His revels to keep,
We sup and we dine,
On seven Score Sheep,
Fat Bullocks and Swine.

*The stairs at the deanery, St Patrick's. Swift exercised
by running up and down these stairs.*

Usquebaugh to our Feast
In Pails was brought up,
An Hundred at last,
And a Madder our Cup.

FINAL YEARS

As he reached his seventies Swift's deafness grew worse. He complained that the noise in his head was intolerable and that he was 'never a day without frequent terrors of a fit of giddiness'. He was afraid to go out in case he fell in the street and instead exercised by running up and down the stairs in the deanery umpteen times a day. Because of his deafness he found conversation difficult and gradually withdrew from seeing his friends. He became irritable, lonely and withdrawn. Sadly, when his great friend Tom Sheridan came to stay at the deanery during one of his bouts of gloom, Swift fought with him and threw him out. Poor Sheridan was very distressed by this and died within weeks.

In May 1740 Dean Swift made his will, leaving a large legacy to found a 'hospital in or near the city, for the support of idiots and lunatics'. Of his bequest he wrote:

He left what little wealth he had
To build a House for Fools and Mad,
And shewed by one satyric Touch,
No Nation wanted it so much.

The founding of St Patrick's Hospital was a kindly and generous gesture as there was no place to care for the insane in Swift's time. Insanity was at the time considered a punishment from God and the insane were often mocked and jeered at in the streets. Even worse, Swift had been a governor of

Swift's desk and watch.

71

the Bedlam Asylum in London where the public, for a few pence, could go in and laugh at the patients. He hated this and hoped it would not be allowed to happen at St. Patrick's. He foresaw the day when the mentally ill would be treated with the same dignity as the physically ill. St Patrick's Hospital is still a thriving and enlightened institution and is often called Swift's Hospital.

Gradually Swift's memory began to fail and in 1742 he was declared incapable of looking after himself. He was put under the care of Rev. John Lyon who managed his affairs for the next three years. Swift was for many years believed to have become insane but medical opinion now says that he suffered from Ménière's Disease, and his frequent complaints throughout his life about giddiness and deafness tie in with this claim.

Dean Jonathan Swift died on 19 October 1745. When the news of his death spread, people wept in the streets of Dublin. Thousands of the population came to see him laid out in an open coffin at the deanery. He was buried three days later in St Patrick's Cathedral, side by side with his much-loved Stella. A black marble tablet on the wall above his grave bears the Latin epitaph he composed. The poet W.B. Yeats freely translated it as:

> Swift has sailed into his rest;
> Savage indignation there
> Cannot lacerate his breast.
> Imitate him, if you dare,
> World-besotted traveller; he
> Served human liberty.

BIBLIOGRAPHY

Bowles Daly, J., *Ireland in the Days of Dean Swift* (London 1887)

Campbell Mary, *Lady Morgan* (London 1988)

Donoghue, Denis, *Jonathan Swift: A Critical Introduction* (London 1969)

Jeffares, A. Norman, *Fair Liberty Was All His Cry* (New York 1967)

Jeffares, a. Norman, *Anglo-Irish Literature* (New York 1982)

Johnston, Edith Mary, *Ireland in the Eighteenth Century* (Dublin 1974)

Kenyon, J. P., *Stuart England* (London 1978)

McHugh, Roger and Edwards, Philip, eds., *Jonathan Swift, 1667-1967, a Dublin Tercentenary Tribute* (Dublin 1967)

Nokes, David, *Jonathan Swift* (London 1987)

Ó hÓgáin, Daithí, *The Hero in Irish Folk History* (Dublin)

Plumb, J.H., *England in the Eighteenth Century* (London 1963)

Rouse, A.L., *Jonathan Swift* (London 1975)

Swift, Jonathan, *A Tale of A Tub, The Drapier's Letters, A Modest Proposal, Gulliver's Travels, Journal to Stella, A Proposal for the Universal Use of Irish Manufacture...*

Tucker, Bernard, *Jonathan Swift* (Dublin 1983)

Williams, Harold, *The Poems of Jonathan Swift* (Oxford 1958)

Williams, Kathleen. ed., *Swift: The Critical Heritage* (London 1970)

Wyse Jackson, Rev. R., *Swift and His Circle*, (Dublin 1945)

Vickers, Brian, ed., *The World of Jonathan Swift: Essays for the Tercentenary* (London 1968)

PLACES TO GO AND THINGS TO SEE

Hoey's Court – street where Swift was born.

Christ Church Cathedral – Swift was ordained in this church.

The deanery, St Patrick's Cathedral – Swift lived here for many years.

St Patrick's Cathedral – Swift served in the cathedral as dean. There are memorials to Swift, Stella, O'Carolan, Boyle and Schomberg, Swift's pulpit table and chair, a collection of his works, a scroll he received as freeman of the city of Dublin and the chair on which King William sat during the Thanksgiving Ceremony for his victory at the Battle of the Boyne.

The Cabbage Garden – top of Cathedral Lane. Swift loved to work in this garden which he once owned.

Marsh's Library – the oldest library in Ireland, founded in Swift's lifetime. It lies between the deanery and the cathedral in Cathedral Close.

Trinity College – Swift was a student at the university. The college has Swift's books, manuscripts, personal papers, as well as a bust and a portrait of him.

Mansion House – the Lord Mayor's chain of office was given by King William to Vanessa's father, Vanhomrigh, when he was Lord Mayor.

Dublin Castle – Swift lived at the castle when he was chaplain to the Lord Lieutenant and he was entertained there many times when he was dean of St Patrick's.

Howth Castle – Swift dined there regularly.

Sandymount Strand – Swift liked to exercise his horses on the strand.

Phoenix Park – Swift often rode in the park. He wrote the following on the magazine fort which still stands in the park:

> Behold a proof of Irish Sense
> Here Irish wit is seen
> When nothing's left that's worth defence,
> We build a magazine.

St Patrick's Hospital – this hospital was founded by Swift.

Dr Steeven's Hospital – Stella left her money to this hospital.

CO. ANTRIM

Kilroot – Swift's first parish.

CO. ARMAGH

Market Hill, now Gosford Castle – Swift often stayed here for long holidays.

CO. CAVAN

Quilca – Tom Sheridan lived here and Swift spent many holidays with him.

CO. DERRY

Derry – the famous walls that held so well during the siege can still be seen.

CO. KILDARE

Celbridge – Swift often visited Vanessa here. There is a bridge in the town known as Swift's Bridge.

CO. KILKENNY

Kilkenny College – Swift was a pupil at the college

CO. LIMERICK

Treaty Stone – the spot that marks the end of the siege of Limerick.

CO. LOUTH

Drogheda – Battle of the Boyne took place about three miles above Drogheda.

CO. MEATH

Laracor – Swift was rector at Laracor. Only the graveyard now remains.

Trim, St Mary's Abbey – the house was once owned by Stella and later by Swift. At the Heritage Centre there is a model of Swift's cottage which was situated just outside the town.

Wood Park – the home of Swift's friend Charles Ford. Swift was a regular visitor to the house.

DATE	SWIFT	IRELAND	WORLD
1667	Swift born in Dublin, 30 November.		Isaac Newton making important scientific discoveries and inventions. Rembrandt painting masterpieces. Milton publishes *Paradise Lost*.
1669	Nurse takes Swift to England. Remains there 3 years.		
1670			Dryden appointed Poet Laureate.
1671		Second English Navigation Act restricts Irish trade.	
1673	Swift, age 6, goes to Kilkenny College.		
1674		Robert Boyle (discoverer of 'Boyle's Law') establishes that metals increase in weight when oxidised.	
1680			Dodo in Mauritius becomes extinct through over-hunting.
1681		Execution of Oliver Plunkett in London.	First bank cheques used in England.
1682	Enters Trinity College, Dublin.		Haley observes the comet which bears his name.
1685			James II becomes King of England.

Year	Swift's life	Irish events	World events
1687		Earl of Tyrconnell appointed lord deputy.	
1688			William of Orange invited to rule England. Dampier explores Australia.
1689	Graduates with BA degree. Leaves Ireland to join his mother in Leicester.	James II lands in Ireland. The Siege of Derry. Jacobite war.	Peter the Great becomes Czar of Russia.
1690		William III defeats James II at the Battle of the Boyne.	
1691	Meets Stella at Moor Park.	Treaty of Limerick.	
1695	Ordained a priest at Christ Church Cathedral, Dublin. Given the parish of Kilroot near Belfast.	Penal laws passed	
1696	Swift returns to Moor Park.		
1698		William Molyneux publishes his famous pamphlet: *The Case of Ireland's being bound by acts of parliament in England stated.*	Newton calculates the speed of sound.
1699	Sir William Temple dies. Swift appointed chaplain to the Earl of Berkeley.		
1700	Becomes vicar of Laracor near Trim, Co. Meath.	Population of Ireland, 2 million.	Pop.:England and Scotland 7m, Hapsburg Empire 7m, Spain 6m.

1701	Back in England Swift publishes his first political pamphlet. Stella and Mrs Dingley come to live in Ireland.	War of the Spanish Succession begins.
1702	Takes Doctor of Divinity Degree at Trinity College, Dublin.	Duke of Marlborough becomes Captain General of English army.
1703		Peter the Great of Russia founds the city of St Petersburg (now Leningrad).
1704	Publishes *A Tale of a Tub*.	
1707	Goes to England on behalf of the Church of Ireland to negotiate remission of the tax known as First Fruits.	Act of Union unites England and Scotland as Gt. Britain.
1708	Begins friendship with Addison and Steele and publishes *Beckerstaff Papers*.	
1709	Meets Esther Vanhomrigh (Vanessa). Fails to gain First Fruits and returns to Ireland.	Battle of Malplaquet. Bad harvests throughout Europe cause famine and food riots.
1710	Succeeds in First Fruits mission. Supports anti-war campaign.	Bishop Berkeley from Kilkenny, famous philosopher, publishes his *Principles of Human Knowledge*. Tories come to power in Britain. St Paul's Cathedral completed in London.

1712	Forms lifelong friendship with Alexander Pope.	Building commences on Trinity College Library.	Last execution for witchcraft takes place in England.

1712	Forms lifelong friendship with Alexander Pope.	Building commences on Trinity College Library.	Last execution for witchcraft takes place in England.
1713	Appointed dean of St Patrick's Cathedral, Dublin.		Treaty of Utrecht ends War of Spanish Succession.
1714	Helps form the Scriblerus Club. Vanessa follows Swift to Ireland.		Queen Anne dies and George I becomes king. Handel writes *The Water Music*.
1717		Building commences on Dr Steeven's Hospital.	Prussia first European country to make school attendance compulsory.
1719		Toleration Act for Protestant dissenters.	First English cricket match. Daniel Defoe publishes *Robinson Crusoe*.
1720	Publishes *A Proposal for the Universal Use of Irish Manufacture* …		
1721			Sir Robert Walpole becomes Britain's first prime minister. J.S. Bach writes *Brandenburg Concertos*.
1722		William Wood purchases patent to coin copper halfpence for circulation in Ireland.	
1723	Vanessa dies, leaves her fortune to Berkeley, the philosopher.		

1724	Publishes the *Drapier's Letters*.	Turlough O'Carolan, the chief musician of Gaelic Ireland publishes 20 tunes in the first-known collection of traditional music.
1725	Swift now known as 'The Hibernian Patriot'. Wood's patent withdrawn	
1726	Publishes *Gulliver's Travels*.	Voltaire's writings causing controversy in London.
1727	Visits England for last time.	
1728	Stella dies on 28 January.	
1729	Shocks the country with *A Modest Proposal*.	Foundation stone laid for the new parliament building in College Green (now the Bank of Ireland).
1736	Publishes 'The Legion Club'.	First appendicitis operation performed.
1737		*Belfast Newsletter* first printed.
1742	Declared to be of unsound mind.	Handel's *Messiah* performed for the first time in Fishamble Street, Dublin.
1745	Dies on 19 October.	Celsius invents the centigrade thermometer.